OUR TONGUES ARE SONGS

By the same author:

Bone Ink

OUR TONGUES ARE SONGS

RICO CRAIG

RECENT
WORK
PRESS

Our Tonges are Songs
Recent Work Press
Canberra, Australia

Copyright © Rico Craig, 2021

ISBN: 9780645008920 (paperback)

 A catalogue record for this
book is available from the
National Library of Australia

Cover image by Joshua Rivera via unsplash
Cover design by Recent Work Press
Set by Recent Work Press

recentworkpress.com

PL

pax, always proud of your heart and wisdom

Contents

with my mates

for Bilal

just going out with my mates
just going to the park
won't be late
just doing some stuff you don't
need to worry about
just want to say i'll be okay
just want to say you don't need every detail
just want to say there'll be girls
just want to say
none of us are stupid
just want to say there are no gangs
just want to say you shouldn't
believe what's on tv
just want to say the radio is worse
just want to say they treat you different
when you're with a group of friends
just want to say
they line us up against a wall
just want to say they empty
our pockets on the ground
just want to say sometimes they whisper
in our ears
just want to say it sounds like fear
just want to say sometimes you can feel
flecks of spit on your neck
just want to say sometimes it's better
to keep quiet
just want to say sometimes it's better to run
just want to say there are places to hide
just want to say
stay in the shadows
just want to say i keep my eyes open
just want to say i'm safe Ma
i'm safe

When parks were still parks

When I come into your life I'll bring a homemade disco ball,
I will wreath my hair in fairy lights, portable speakers
will sprout from my hands, and gin will flow thick and cool
from a hole in my side. You'll know the right words but hide
them in the palm of your hand. I'll be whirling
and gossiping in three tongues, wearing a digital watch

that always tells the wrong time. This is
the year of visible breath, our friends threaten
to keep us from each other. Every party we promise
to fall in love with another person. It never happens,
In the future we're already laughing about the days
we melted holes in plastic bottles, cut clothes

into threats and threw lipgloss at passing trains.
We have twenty-six songs and I play them
on a loop whenever we're apart. We have precise calculations
to make; when to look up, the right bus to catch,
what to hide in our bags. I'm coming to you, I'm on Crystal
Street, the bus is late, people are waving at taxis;

this is the first day of the second apocalypse, lights flash
on Parra Rd. Meet me at the gazebo in Elkington Park,
wait for me, stay there, wait for me;
wear your shirt with the white pinpricks,
forget your bag and carry everything you need
in your arms—there's nothing worth rescuing

from the hours they prop us at tables and make us brag.
There are kids on this bus spitting on each other,
some of them are rapping into paper bags.
The scrunching of paper sounds like a lover's hex,
like your voice saying—take my hand, remember
the grass, the dirt, remember kicking those empty bottles.

Our better selves are disobedient

Teenagers march the streets
in silence, red flags propped
on shoulders, tape across their lips.

It's the last day of free speech
and they're arm to arm
doing some palm-to-palm

dance from the seventeenth century.
I have no idea how this knowledge
came into their legs.

All the buses slow, we watch
from the windows and see
shadows under skin.

A nose is bleeding.
Phones don't work—
when people want attention

they flash headlights.
We take notes about days in May,
watch people through binoculars.

The only time I comprehend protest
is when I skim history books. Have I told you
about the dead bodies?

There will be too many.

The ASX pours from your chest

We squabble about the money skimmed
from our drudgery, the barbs lift
enemies from our skin. At the end of shifts
we are lathered in sweat and the day is night;

cars move above us and I have blood on my palms.
Your teeth are broken, we are old
we are the same, we have always been here
we are layers of dried paint. On our best days

we are birds, we are flocks of laughter
we are dawn. When they grind another hour
from your skin, new enemies appear.
They burst from your chest frothing,

phones in fists, plastic in pockets,
they will never hold our eye,
they will talk to our foreheads
they will beat us with chains—

then park outside our house
and wait on the street to mark
our children with their stares.
We will not let them steal us

we will turn them inside out
we will feast on their feebleness
we will make ourselves sharp
we will slide an answer
into their throat.

When the towers fall

Cook and Matavai

Out the window there's a hole, one yellow crane bends against the sky. Our pasts pour into trucks, somewhere panels are being added to light rail carriages, the timetable to another place is being talked about, transit, anti-graf seats, the inoculation of whir and motion, filtered air. I'm coughing now. I have been for weeks, the paint is peeling from my throat.

Turanga and Solander

It's difficult to speak with dust in the air, words struggle to leave us. Mostly we wait in corridors and point. When people aren't at our door with hammers we talk about the objects designed to make us talk. When notices aren't taped across hallways, we laugh. When the elevators listen we move through air like a feather falling.

Marton and Banks

There are six ravens telling us the towers are ready to fall. In the bathroom we gather around empty containers, the plastics of a lifetime, the confected scents of cucumber, its promise to glimmer, rough soap that loses its shape. We gather them and plot restitution. If we leave it will be slowly, four centimetres each year.

Lunar Retreat

i.

Everything I own waits on the footpath, my window
is cracked. The only name I'm allowed to use is written
on stickers. I don't know the writing. All I own
is less than four squares of pavement.

In the archway Andrea from the third floor
is slamming the entrance door back on itself,
with each swing the hinges stretch. The air
burns. I watch her lose energy, there's only

space for fear and voices. We're being
carried from this place, we walk in small circles
around everything we own. Moths taunted by possession.

ii.

I hold two forks in my right hand, shake them at the sky,
there's too much blue, too many cranes. We're shapes
filled with colour, waiting to become soot.

There are parts of me standing on rooftops,
my fingernails are fallen leaves, this chest
is a sliding glass door, my walls are thin.

When I fall it will be with this building. Our sorry
birds are leaving the towers, they're made of smoky
air, claws of aluminium foil. I feel them scratching

on my arms, their talons take grip, cut holes
in my sleeves, break the surface, steady into my skin.
They lift me from the ground and I am

in the air with a thousand birds
and they purr as the smoke of their wings
lifts me. We rise above the windows

and for the first time in decades my bones feel
hollow, light and ready for air.

iii.

On the new moon I sharpen my boyfriend,
cut myself a ragged fringe, hold him
to my leg, boreal and ruthless.

*—meet me at headz up the barber down from where dominos was bring your eftpos
card bring some money i need to tell you something did you get the letter they were
pushing under everyones door—*

I parade the streets, run with him by my side;
name and bind him in a sheet for five days. At dawn
we chalk messages on street poles, arrows, question marks;
rendezvous in parking lots, love letters behind our hands.

—i heard them talking at the meeting the other day if were still here in a week
theyre going to send in people to help us pack im not sure what that means maybe
everything you own gets chucked in a skip maybe they put your stuff in boxes and
dont put labels on them—

On the new moon I sharpen my boyfriend. We lay
in the shadow of an overpass, sleeping against walls,
ravens circle our heads. I place him between my teeth
and climb. The ravens shy and lift away. Headlights flash
and from the overpass I show my blade
to passing cars. I am dangerous in this place
people will make one hundred calls to keep me safe.

Mathematics of the future

In the bleakest of hours
statistics turn into a vision machine of birth and death.
People talk about dollars
dry-humping the exponentials of superannuation.

Our visionaries are bespectacled, paunchy and unable
to comprehend heartbeats.
There are economists wrapping

their tongues in foil,
they're calling the sky purple
and telling us to invest in the truth.
Interest is secure, dollars multiply.

It has nothing to do with chance,
everything is organisation
and logistics.

Futures are spiders made of air
they bind whole worlds,
dewdrops and light on thread,
and when we rest it is on silken webs.

Paper skull

'the you in most of my poems is myself'
Duy Quang Mai

Your skull is made from paper. Everything you know
comes from a pinterest board, your philosophers
are youtube conspirators. We don't ever talk to each other.
I'm listing nervous tics and miscalculations. Your grey rage

tells me something has been said at the wrong time.
Words like 'love' mean learning lines, creating sets,
employing costume designers, makeup artists
and sending producers with sandpapered nostrils

to search the world for locations. Rumours say you live
in a new time, there are no clocks, only a haze—
neither day or night. Let's agree to talk with our fingers,
in a midnight room, with our best friends projected ghoulish

on screens. We can be backlit into permanence.
Let's drive through the coal dust and ash,
weave around trucks, find a way into the hills
where we can hide in what remains of trees and grass.

Each new day is made from burnt leaves and the moon's
dead smile. Covered in the material of clouds, we'll sleep
on the grass and wait for the world to slow around us.
We're starting to believe our friends might be beautiful, they draw

pictures in monochrome. Every day colours cease to be
and we realise—if we're still—we can be the shape of things to come.

Butterflies in the green belt

we live leaning into curves   there are no straight roads in our suburb
cars sway through roundabouts   the creek is a busted tap   every journey circuitous
each day an indirect threat   shops have one of everything   BWS sells to infants
what we wish for is around the next corner   i haven't seen a footpath in days
the only place to walk is the bike track   we pretend that isn't bad

when i see other humans i don't even shout hello   we know it will be the same time
same place every day   we have our routines   and what isn't routine
is dictated by renovation jobs and time spent waiting in telephone queues
hearing voices that pledge attentiveness and register every flutter
our heart makes   we share our broken parts again and again
only to discover the line is empty

we're kissing cold screens   the roads are better friends
we're all killers walking bike tracks   we do push-ups in the exercise area and genocide
falls from the trees   each brake squeal becomes a voice   each broken blade of grass
a word people don't notice   we scream in parklands   essay the creek
chant each night as insects rub their legs together

Each night my suit remembers how to dance

We dance with knives in our hands,
we fight with taffeta
over our eyes.

Don't tell me how many times
I cut you and if
this wet on my hands is blood.

I can hear your breath talking,
we're backtracking from reality.
In the morning there's a residue

truth has left wondering on our tongues.
Behind you there's a balcony
and beyond,

across the road, first light
on a terrace. We've forgotten
the quaint modesty of underwear,

you're the colour fingers leave
on a throat.
Our secrets are a mosquito coil smoking.

My suit has lost a button. We promised
this would be the last time.
I've smoked everything except

your eyelashes. Last time
I looked there were diamonds
in your sink—

I think they're broken glass.
I'm always meant to be here.
You're breathing toward the balcony.

Gravity is too sincere;
When I call the ambulance
they want to know what happened,

I tell them you have blood
in your ears,
and then I think,

it must be hard to hear through liquid.
Your eyes are filled with street light,
there are moths in morning turmoil.

No gin in the afternoon

There are no crystal glasses,
no gin in the afternoon.
I've stopped wearing eyeliner
beneath my right eye. There's nothing

worth flagging. On winter days
I take out the suit I wore
the night we met. First time—
I went out bare, shirt-less

under the dinner suit—fifty bucks
from Jazz Garter. You grabbed me
by the silk lapels, I can count
the places I wore it with you.

My husband is a blind giant,
dancing to what can never be. I married
myself into a handshake. The suit
is hidden in a bag

he doesn't think about. He and I
eat crackers between meals,
anything to stop us from talking.
I spend whole days with crumbs

on my chin. I can't rake them off.
He doesn't notice. There are things
we don't talk about, the ever-after,
the colour of my hair,

the car in the drive without wheels.
It becomes too much.
When I direct taxis home, this address
is a curse I force myself to utter.

So many words don't belong
in my mouth. Now, in sunlight, this suit
looks old, like it's waiting for your moths,
waiting to hold the body I knew you with.

Ten breaths

Our favourite lovers are raging at the night, they litter
the ground with threats. A lifetime consists of ten breaths;
without gravity we would float in space and everything
would be serene. We're in the kitchen and garlic is frying slowly,

melting, we can't stop talking. In the time we trade fears
there's a thicker scent. In a breath flesh will loosen,
the streets will turn to winter wind. In a breath
talcum powder drifts white reminders
across a grandmother's floor. In a breath
days perch on shoulders and peek
between strands of hair. In a breath one hundred daughters
dance their doubts into dust. In a breath friends scrawl
condolences in the dark. In a breath life is hollowed
by hashtags. In a breath we case futures
and they surge toward us, sun at their back,
waving spoons. In a breath your hand claws
and I clutch my chest. In a breath we're older. In a breath

we hear answers, we speak over breakfast,
we promise there will be an afternoon,
we discuss the best place to catch our lovers
as they leap at us from passing trains.

There are various narrative arcs in seasons 5, 6 and 7 of *Full House* that remain unresolved

Twenty-four episodes in season six

When I was hospitalised for six months
they tortured me with bananas, Bega cheese
and seasons 5, 6 and 7 of Full House.
We watched from lounge chairs, our arms

wrapped in Nirvana t-shirts. To stay warm
and slender was a craft,
the only skin we showed the world

was face. The Tanner sisters crossed
their legs, pouting, dagger-staring, bleeding

normality from every cracked lip.

A list of things that tell me it's time to rewatch Full House

Counting in sevens is the only thing
that keeps the lounge room in focus. My heart
is filled with shoelaces. For a long time
I eat only the question marks
served to me. There is nothing bite-sized

every forkful is an endless tomorrow. I shave
fluff from my arms. I want to save each strand
in a jar. There are things to master;
walk straight, don't fall, don't look

people in the eye, know when traffic
lights change, look to the right.
Be careful stepping off kerbs.

Know the world is moving through space
and there is nothing we can imagine

that will stop dawn from coming.

In the house with my golden-haired sisters

The Olsen twins and I cohabitate; white pickets
surround the house. They're teen obsessives hoarding
recycling and talking about quinoa salads. Cars are u-turning
in the street out front, cruising; people hang

phones out their windows. This place is Gram-friendly,
I've been burning holes in the carpet with fire-starters
patch by patch until my heart is a bed of ash. No one

knows what's going on in here. They're looking
at the window dressing. We have underpants hanging

from door handles, classic rock playing.

Full House season 5 episode 16

At least once a year the sisters lick spatulas
covered in chocolate cake, drive across the bridge
in a convertible, sometimes wear blazers
to the park and sit around a picnic basket. We sway

when visitors arrive. Birthday parties are the closest
we come to a forest. I'm eternally tempted by toffee apples
and denim jackets. Some of my friends look like skeletons.

There are shoe boxes filled with forgotten souvenirs;
on the bedroom shelf—strange self-help books—101 Ways

To Help Children Like Themselves.

Full House season 7 episode 17

Bay window prison, red door; emotional racketeers
around the kitchen table, plotting through cheeks of food.
Kids beaming beneath makeup, holding apples,
wearing sunglasses inside. Walls are an excuse
for hagiography and heraldic life lessons; we pledge

with our mouths closed, clash teeth to keep ourselves
empty. I'm considering a centre part. Every old man
is a doctor, is like Santa Claus without a beard,
they put flour on your nose and dispense wisdom. If I learn

to dance it will be in the lounge room rocking a pant suit.
We're all wearing scrunchies, even when our eyes
are full of death. We walk the halls with ponytails swinging.

If I'm about to cry I tilt my head to the right
and cover my eyes with a fist. We're looking for answers

from people who have ears too low on their skull.

When the family from *Full House* appears at my bed

during season seven all i eat is fish roe
it's a constraint that lasts
until the ambulance arrives
i've got blood in my palm and people
cover me with a blanket
i know who they are
tv sisters with blond hair
laughter more obvious
than the Golden Gate
i've been watching them
lick their lips and pout
i know they're here to help me
there have been worse things than this
my housemates speak like knotted hair
i secret food in thimbles
i'd hide jars in the overgrown garden
so no one thinks about me
except my sisters and their glass eyes
they tell me when it's safe to eat
i've been teaching them to sing Tunic
they only listen to bands with guitars
i sing it to them now
as they wheel me from the house

Recovery Hotel

55 Kilograms
For three months twins have been pinching my torso,
my thighs, the back of my arms. They have told me
hour after hour to eat nothing
except fish roe from the Russian Deli
to know only the tender buoyancy of bubble
after bubble between my incisors. I balance
each egg on a toothpick, tip it onto my tongue.
The twins look at me like I'm royalty,
as they stub their cigarettes out
in pizza boxes.

54 Kilograms
This is called an ailment by some people; he's wilful
is what people say behind my back. I notice.
Every day is a bubble on my tongue.

53 Kilograms
I'm wearing shapeless frocks
handed down from my grandmother,
sometimes overalls, I'm like a snake
in a laundry basket. Everything fits
and nothing is right.

52 Kilograms
My bible is a book full of calories;
it's natural to count and pay
attention to the world
as it enters.

51 Kilograms
Everything is better than before. This is
what people call recovery,
this is past stage two. I'm making
my own decisions, this is not even
losing weight. I am a needle
in a haystack, sharp enough
to find your eye.

48 Kilograms
This ceiling is a cartography,
this ceiling should have tidal charts.
I've been across this mercator projection,
tumbled into the void between seas.
My answers are anchor marks on the shoreline
and I am an argument with the ocean.

Recovery Hotel
each morning i wake   skinny as the reed
my sleep breathes into song   i've been dreaming
my pinch test twins   are both alive   living in room 31
with a plastic bag   to hold their clothes   sharing dresses

they front the world with L'Oréal smeared on their foreheads
it's always Ash Wednesday   except hair dye   there's nothing
to convince me   this isn't true   i don't know where the hotel is
there's the smell of fried fish   salads with banana and chilli

my twins know all the patients in this place   they enter and exit lobbies
the floor is a marble continent   gold brocade blocks the sun
leather shrieks like a small animal   when we recline   there are ostriches crossing
a grassed plain on the wall   our better-life is adolescent-colonial

near the check-in desk a patron spins the globe   it speeds until countries blur
all the halls are full of brittle people   talking about socials
and superfood recipes   we're healthy as string beans   vacuum sealed
we gossip like a plague of bones   we're sharp blades

covered in down   our minds are addled with crossword clues
our mouths synonym machines   glitzed with a coat of lipgloss
growling new words for   hunger   desire   theft   this world
is a banquet of misnomers   scribbled notes balled and dropped in corridors

our necks are covered in love bites   teaspoons hidden
behind wardrobes   shots of cactus nectar every morning   i'm sleep walking
the halls   i see silver numbers at dawn   i never knock
my twins rough their hands together   and open the door   there are no sounds

in this world   no one speaks   a mouth is only for reunion with a better self
questions don't desire air   even daylight has become doubtful

the floor is mopped eight times an hour   and dust gathers on every surface
somehow they have a room   we discuss granite colonnades

a door made of teak   we have been entangled for 1000 meals
my footsteps tap messages on the marble   the morning-light is a bird
with a razor   in its beak   my twins lie to me   in the language of insects
there is nothing in the air to soothe   our compulsions

and when we rest the moon waits for us in the hills   out the window
i reckon with clouds   and the names my twins gave me
we have come to this place   to be made safe
they serve sunlight on a white plate   we feast without shadows

Inamorato

I've been riding pillion with you, precious cargo, leaves
lifting from the roadside as we pass. My love is bedlam,
it arrives like a blind horde and threatens
to leave French without an adieu. At hotels we hide
behind doors; by midday it feels safe enough
to lift food from plates. Each evening we pet golden dogs—
neither fox nor wolf—as they suckle
furless babies, new worlds whimpering. Multitudes pass,
searching for songs that have no chorus, pictures
that have no people. We want to escape to a house
carved from a single piece of wood. I want the tree
to grow around me. You want to perch on a wooden heartbeat,
breathe like a sparrow. For the first time I am
ready to be bound by rings, ribbed by each year,
protected by bark—my hair swaying branches.
I can speak microcosms; when I move it is slowly,
without footsteps, the earth will shift over me—
wind moving leaves, each grain of dirt another pilgrimage.

Allow passengers to disembark
before boarding

You say the word—   —and I try to see it
in the yellow doors as they slide open. I try to find it
in the strange ping a transit card elicits from the barrier
as we run for a train, in the indicators people forget
to use, in the way pedestrians are compelled to scurry
against the lights. I translate it from the way mini-marts
organise their shelves, the way tissues are hidden
behind biscuits. I notice it in the way grass grows
beneath a park bench. When the sky trawls
toward evening, I agree. The trains continue,
and people standing in rows see,
on the passing glass, their clear selves flicker.

Dancing at the Bone Bank

for bea

Perhaps some things are easier to replace
than others, perhaps we can grow
in ways that have intent. What I'm talking about
is called healing. It's done with the hardest
parts of our body—along the walls

protecting our blood machines,
but I'm drifting
and as we speak
osteoblasts are forming
and I am becoming more than I was.

Maybe Bone Bank is misleading. The place
I imagine
has tellers wearing latex gloves,
there are no sounds,
every transaction is the hush scree makes above the tree line.

On the walls,
like the names of gods we mustn't forget,
are the words:
OSTEOGENESIS
OSTEOINDUCTION
OSTEOCONDUCTION

I understand
that the prefix 'osteo' has something
to do with the shapes that lurk
beneath my skin.
I also understand the words:
degradation
process
harvesting.

These seem less important.

I know most donations
come from femoral heads
removed during hip replacements. I know
osteoconduction is the process
whereby a piece of toner bone
is used to create a bridge
or guide, along which the patient's osteoid
substance grows. Mostly I try
not to think about the other bones
in my body.

I tell you this because I am the host,
a walker of bridges
and I am growing as dictated.
This is called healing,
it's a function of the body.

I'm told not to think about the healing
process
except when I'm told to concentrate
on the healing process—to imagine my osteoid
substance painting itself over a strip of stranger's bone,
coat upon coat,
endlessly
and somewhere in this process
the pain will leave me.

There are changes I will notice
and there will be others
that occur without announcement.
This is called recovery,
this is what the future looks like, this is one reason
people worry about time passing.

The bones are stored at minus eighty-five degrees Celsius.
I imagine a room like a vault,
filled with metal boxes, I imagine
velvet gloves, ear muffs
and the metallic sliding made
when professionals extract a safe deposit box

from a wall of safe deposit boxes.
Inside there are bones of various size and shape
some are still grimed with human flesh,
there are bulbs of tendon and cartilage.
This is what people call medicine.

Soon a professional will select
the bone that is most suitable for me. There will be
no discussion. The bone will be removed
from a metal box
it will be placed in a sterilised receptacle,
sterilised instruments
will be used to hone the shape
required to actuate the osteoconductive process.
Bones need motivation
and guidance.

On winter days I will be able to sense
the cold fragments of bone beneath my skin.
This is what people call clarity.

In unfamiliar cities I will find myself
standing outside the Bone Bank. Inevitably
the bank will have Doric columns,
it will be built from buffed grey stone;
people will enter and exit a swinging glass door.
Security guards will have their hands
crossed over belt buckles. I never enter,
I stand for a few minutes
thinking of the memories concealed by skin
and somewhere in me I feel the bones
dance for their true home.

Calico shadows

There are walls around this city and the protection
a half moon of water provides. Rooms are full of strange
furniture and children's clothes blow from the balcony.

Our shadows move through hidden rooms,
up spiral stairs, when the sun is almost blue with its love
for the sky. The hills are schist, garrigue and debris;

our bus winds an ant track through Flowering Ash.
When we arrive at the city gates it's almost midnight,
there are steps and fountains, the calcified

remains of a deer herd. Our shadows are shapes
collecting keys from a pizza shop, we are the coils of shade
making handprints on limestone walls. Our touch fills

the darkness with holes, and for a few nights we believe
in ramparts, tell secrets to peacocks and our hearts
murmur, two sighs from sleep.

Centro

We're the child in a restaurant kitchen
trying to dance with waiters.

Smiling a question and laugh-swaying
with arms crossed. These aproned men

lead us to the footpath and twirl
us back to seats; the streets around Centro

have a memory for dance steps, after dusk
there are a thousand people reaching for hands.

Nights promise a taxi ride and the stutter
language leaves against this hot air.

We wash concrete dust down the drains,
hide from bees on rooftops. We drink

Fanta every day. There are some things
that never change; we are here

to remind the heat we were here.
All the buildings are half-finished

or half-destroyed. We're waiting
for builders to wake and finish the job

they've started. The whole city is stoic
and restive, riding tiny buses,

all buying bread from the same store,
flipping coins at fountains.

La Pineta

They arrive wandering, map-lost, down the hill
into a grove of pines, near the dust a football ground spills,

tomorrow the stands will be filled with a thousand voices
screaming at legs and leather. Their hotel has an empty lobby,

they trail sand, sit on lounges and wonder
if people will ever appear, if this is another lobby

where a person waits forever to make eye contact
with every sin they'll commit. They sit on vinyl,

staring. There's space for a bus outside, it must be
arriving soon. They test telephones on the lobby table,

look at dreams the '70s built from plastic—
and what they've done with them now, all the collapsed

edges and moulded approximations of comfort.
Beyond the drive, a dirt road leads past a fire pit

and up the steps into town. There's the smell
boiled sea creatures make as they die

and pine nettles and the aluminium siding
caravans angle at the sun. The sea doesn't

believe in waves and they float in the salty soup
then sleep with sand on their feet, cliff-side

graffiti under their eyelids. In their dreams
the sun sets inland and they watch the incoming

ocean make islands of the peninsula.

A shape wind carves in night

Sun-fall marks the end of our vision
dry oceans surround us, sand toiling in rivulets.
Colours change. There's a silver platter
beside my knee, above us, past the edge of town,

the longest dune, a spine along this continent,
begins. We wait for the wind, wait for sand
to rise off the dune in shapes we know.
The wind is always blowing, every day

people are swallowed by sands, each footstep
summons a skeleton. We pour tea, the sky is
mustard and blue. There are four-wheel drives churning
the dunes, overloaded with people. I reach for

a plate of almonds, scrape them across the silver
and the sky begins to change, a four-wheel drive slides down
the side of a dune. We're waiting for darkness,
a series of spotlights to celebrate the end.

We pour more mint tea, I spoon sugar, we talk
about fumes, scents, streams. There are times we almost forget.

Carlsbad Caverns, New Mexico:
all the cold nights are one night

My legs are open, like the fist you lay across me
palm down, finger prints rippling
across my belly. There's crystal
on the windscreen, the first frost of morning.

I watch the moonlight fracture
into stories. You're huffing hot breath
at them. Your hands have mostly known me
better. This is what we planned. It reminds me

how November wind tastes like ice. How we can live
on toast and honey for a whole winter. I don't know
how long we've been waiting in New Mexico for the cold
to settle in our bones. Below the Carlsbad surface

we search each of the 119 caves, with their Devil Springs,
Whale Mouths and Frozen Waterfalls—this is our anniversary,
you still love me, but we can no longer talk
about children, instead we pitch tents, follow trails

and fill our minds with geology's guano and the empty promises
made by unborn babies. We could have been here
with different skin on our bones, different words
to say. This morning when I climbed out of your hold

there was water frozen in tin cups, our fire
was the colour dew leaves on ash and our scars
were nuzzling in the half-light of a wailing child.

Chiroptera: Seven Ages of Juliane Koepcke

& Juliane is reborn through clouds, with a polished coin
under her tongue, no wings. Lightning scrawls history
on the sky; bats cradle her falling, each scream swaddled
in leathery wings. Metal, fire and loved bodies cascade;
her brief infancy is sonar—screeches and rushing air.

& Juliane opens her eyes; the earth reaching for her, arms green
and clothed in leaves, vines twisting and snaking, branches running
through her hair. There is a bone outside her skin, she has been born
from the deepest sleep. Her lips bite together, fish move in the river
confessing water. She learns to walk, lets the mud hold her ankles.

& Juliane moves along the river with a branch in her hand, pushing
from the banks. There are creatures squirming in the red
under her skin. She has doused them in fluid from a metal can.
People are lusting from the shoreline, waiting for her to breathe
so they can write words in newspapers and fill screens with light.

& Juliane escapes to the lawns gripping university buildings; twenty years,
and all the pages she types are bound with fig and fructose.
People cannot hold a conversation with awe; she cannot love people
who drape her body in gowns. She longs for a cloud roiling
with bats, their yawning wings, their faith in science.

& Juliane is a tiny body cradled in the membrane of decades. The bats gnaw
at nocturnes. She stalks caves, listening for the echo of flight, painting
yellow words on wings as they sleep. The bones in her arms are thin
as starlight, longing to be marrowed. Each evening a thousand bats
swirl from the cave-mouth and never worry a hair on her body.

& Juliane flutters eyelashes and people see immortality, a wild man
pretends to wear her skin. He looks at the sky for raining metal
and fills her pockets with chess pieces, promising they represent
something—a way to persist. She sifts through
bat waste, gathering seeds, looking for scratches made by tiny teeth.

& rainforest trees remember the sound of her breaking bones,
under the canopy there are mounds that could be maternal, flesh taken
by leaves. The forest is always hungry and the river is tireless.
She returns the coin to the place under her tongue and lowers
herself into the river-mud, waiting for her mother to fall from the sky.

Adjustable side rails

For days people have fluttered at the border of my bed,
arched toward my face, said my name. My mother
has been reading me newspapers, enunciating her way
through world news and sporting results. She knows
what it's like to be bed-bound. It doesn't hurt much

at the moment, the painkillers come in swampy waves
for hours I'm floating on knots of seaweed,
counting leaves and the star-dots beyond.
I don't say a word, my hands don't twitch. I'm going
to stay as silent as I can, until I remember

all the things I need to know. My mother still
puts her cheek to mine every time she enters the room.
Sometimes I start to see friends and family,
through my closed eyelids, moving in a red ocean.
They play me music. I don't know why

I don't want to speak, explain why I'm waiting
for the right time. When they grip my hand
I stay slack, let them press fingers against the tendons
inside my wrist. They tell me things
I've been waiting to hear. I've been waiting,

people will grow bored of the breathing.
When they visit there isn't much to say; my mother
continues to read aloud—segments she has
clipped from newspapers and magazines, she hates
reading from her phone. For a week all she read

was short story after short story, some were barely
a story. They made my breath catch. She never said
the name of the author, and I couldn't look.
It was the closest I came to shifting from this stillness.
Can you cry with eyes closed? Sometimes it's hard

to stop myself. I can feel my muscles melting
into the sheets. We're all a day or two from being
wrapped in cloth. I can come out of this whenever
I want, all this practice clinging to the next heartbeat.

Two hearts

His medication comes in three colours,
I'm waiting for the nausea to start—
telling myself sometimes it doesn't. The doctors blink
twice when they take his blood pressure,
it's not even worth repeating the numbers. We cover our minds
in sympathy scars and the lies
paediatric surgeons use to craft sleep.

We whisper incomplete verities, make wishes
to skin-thin organs; there are parts of him
that want to escape. I can't stop
thinking about the parts that run, the parts
that flee a body before they know their leaving
is less than being born. If there were
two hearts beating in my chest,

one could be his and the other would hammer
at life's shape—it would read maps, run
laps of the oval, tell secrets on street corners.
It would be the heart corroding, gummed
with sodium chloride; while his new heart
would gleam, a forty-year-old memory
machine, beating flawless in his chiffon chest.

Waves rising and falling

What I do to get by:

turn the shower on all hot
and sit outside the bathroom
talking to steam

pretend my daughter is selecting fruit
in another room
calling out
about
nectarines and lychees

imagine the cat is still with us
part hidden under the unturned sheets
on an unmade bed

shave off the thinnest curls of butter
and line them in rows
on the kitchen bench

stockpile the grains of liquid
and millilitres of salt

reverse the proportions in a recipe

pour chick peas into a colander
rinse
soak
dry
and repeat—
day after day

Driving down the South Coast

My better mind enters the car with dirt on his feet,
slams the door, rattles the windows. I wish
he'd walk. He has a Casio keyboard under his arm;

to block out the traffic noise he plays single finger
scales. Over and over. Music soothes us
so we must be beasts—isn't that how logic works?

It's difficult to stop being one or the other; I sit
at the steering wheel and try to keep my hands still,
my eyes on the white lines. He's fussing

in the glove box, pulling out the choker
he likes to wear, he looks like some girl
I loved in the eighties. He talks like her

as well; I try to listen but he isn't here for me.
He's just doing the rounds, letting me know
he's here, in the back alley, listening for kids'

voices and no matter how fast I drive
there's no escape. The cold air will come,
soon I'll be walking the house in socks and

there'll be a night my daughter enters middle age,
wraps a towel around her head and reads
the business section of the newspaper to keep her mind

off the flavours people push into her mouth.
He stares at my hands, he knows this is what compels
people to let go of the steering wheel, to find a place

on a section of highway that doesn't have barriers
and to let the car drift a little too far, feel the wheels
lose themselves in loose stones and then the silence

of air, the last of earth falling from the chassis.

Campsites

At night there is nothing familiar,
the sound two boys make breathing,
the words nightmares leave on frost.

Two inches of foam keeps me
from becoming earth. My nephews
cry for help. I don't know the nightmares

people have, the way nocturnal dialects
answer each other. We're in a canvas shroud,
young heart beats flutter

messy wings at the night air.
Each turn in sleep is a feather crumpling;
I long for birds

who have beaten the sky empty.
Every twitch is a lover's
torment. The tent grumps in the wind,

coastal rain on grass,
air is what remains in the headlights,
cars poke around the corners

fearful of children hurtling on bikes.
A grandmother limps
with a metal hip, cane under her hand,

blue cardigan, brooch above her heart;
from the jumble of names in her throat
she beckons another grandchild to the fire.

Dyarubbin: Riddles on the Hawkesbury River

Fists bound in mangrove roots
a garland of oyster shells
looping his brow, Riddles spits a piece of himself at the tide
He hums ancient show tunes and waits
for the river currents under his skin
to stop their shifting.

His thoughts are cradled in the arms of two-stroke
each memory hitched to the drone and splash of an outboard.
Downriver a million strangers burn their lives into heat haze
and his river empties a heart into smug city arms.

Riddles is wet to the knees,
dragging his tinnie through the gentle wave wash.
Behind him the wafer rustle of eucalyptus leaves in the breeze
the glint of windows,
a weekender under the escarpment.
Riddles is watching the house
a plush welt among the gums.

He's been here before, he carries
a few broken body parts
hidden in his mind's hessian sack,
they're the fingers of someone he trusted,
the wrist of the person who turned a blind eye,
the forearm of a man who bit his tongue.

He stares into the glaze of mid-river,
the muscle line of currents
and hums another tune, something
about a place he belongs and he waits
for night to seep across the river.

Lake Eucumbene

Eucumbene has fallen below the stump
our old lives lift their lips through the water
surface to sip air. In the umbrage of our kitchen
my mother is frying trout, there are crumbs
on the bench, flesh sticking to the pan,
butter smokes. She flips the fish
onto a plate, cuts more butter into the pan
it smooths to a quivering pool.
She asks me why I've been so long.

Adaminaby has risen from the water,
my mother has told this story in bubbles
since she passed. We know
there are waves.
When she walks from the room,
I try not to follow.

Outside her kitchen, there's a crumpled church
dying in the mud;
the bag I packed has split open,
my clothes have disappeared,
five decades of silt has covered a stack of dinner plates.

The parts we don't need have been turning into clouds
they open on other lakes
break the surface.
Rush into rivers, fall
into the mouths of fish,
buried in a stomach shaped by gills.

We are fluid as broken promises,
the water recedes before us.
We walk into the mud,
bare feet, graceless ankles, sliding, stones beneath our heels.

Wingen: A gentle incline to Burning Mountain

Veer toward Burning Mountain
let the car palpitate a final time,
roll to a stop in the gravel. It's a relief
to be rid of fuel and the imperative to continue.

There are no other cars. Evening is a shape
above the trees, a dirt path scribes dusty
under leaves. Noise is a name for wind.
As the trees give birth to stars and insects chant

at sunset, let your memory lift leaves and listen.
Let smoke rise through fissures in the earth,
epoch's breath, a haze, bending vision.
This is the place where smoke finds a path

between toes, footprints become a basin of grey.
As the grass understands itself into husks, then dust
and vapour, let yourself walk dry loam's perpetual rasp.
You will tell yourself to burn things for comfort, anything,

even the hairs plucked from another scalp
balanced in an apothecary's bowl, lit
with the blunt end of a flame. When you leave
watch the cooling towers and their wild hair, they are

a pair of eyeless follies ever dancing. Remember you are
not even footprints, you are grass turned on its side.

Snake

A brown snake in two pieces,
its midsection a paste,
still trying to poison the air.

There are hopes that need to be sucked
out and spat on the ground.

The truck is a rumble.
There's a noise in the roadside grass,
wind wanting me to remain attentive.

For Pinuccio Sciola

Bare to the waist, covered in insect bites and mud,
scratched by the scrub we've beaten
a path through. You're beside me
chewing words through a cleft palate
parting mist with bricklayer arms.
We've travelled two days, taken a pre-dawn bus

lashed the air with our arak-breath, to arrive
at this place, on this day. Finally, we're robed
in island light; every trench we've dug, each shovel
we've turned, all the bricks we've carried
have been for the three dawns we'll be
on this plateau fasting sounds from basalt,

our labour groaning toward song.
Beyond where we stand, the escarpment
drops jagged to the ocean, white
water bleeds from the horizon.
We have squandered many mornings,
wasted each equinox on building sites

chalking outlines around shadows—
waiting for light to deny our predictions.
The list of countries we travelled through
is tattooed on my left side; you sit
on a faded Bali, lean on the healing
scab of Italy. We're always the last ink

before parlours close; always avid for blood,
our fingers whittling knives. Now we can
carve our primal pleasures into air, feel the sounds
falling from our hands, our fingers mumble gravel,
they weal and chafe music from basalt slabs.
In these dawns we're human enough to crawl

from the undergrowth; sift through
the scree beneath worked stone
and recognise a marriage proposal,

a novel, three broken friendships,
a cousin with a mouthful of grief—
all that should have been said from sun-fall

to three stars. Now we know
there are places to be ancient: a cliff face
where stones sing and our ribs are the hollow
wind plays through, where we can labour
rocks from their silence, feel our hands hum.

When we forget our pagan songs

You have beads sown in your hair,
fingernails fashioned from tin, there's another dimension
beating in your chest, your earrings are blood-covered silver dollars.

between our fingers

We hide words with laughter and fold
inward. Now could be thirty years ago, I'm talking
to you in a beer garden, in the rain, with cigarettes.

between our fingers

Let's talk about silence,
the breath between desire and realisation,
the empty space in our memory.

between our fingers

When I close my eyes there are distant pagan songs
and the sound white noise makes pretending
to be blood, everything present is shivering to retain shape.

between our fingers

I don't know how you arrived
at this place, real enough to put your hand
on my cheek. Let's talk about the way songs slip

between our fingers.

Under Caraballo Mountains

Tito Pat is weary

Tito Pat is weary, Tito Pat has blisters
on his feet—he has forgotten the name
his grandchildren gave their dog.
Behind him a field fades toward harvest,
the irrigation channels are clogged.
The flatlands have been surveyed
with a notched stick, straight lines marked
with shadow and woven palm fronds.
Goats move on dirt roads, goats speak
to rocks, goats chase the sunset.

Tito Pat looks at the mountains

Tito Pat wants to return to the mountains,
to guide his family through the hills. There are grey hairs
growing from his earlobes, today he starts the morning
with a cold Red Horse, whenever he can he carries ice
in his fist. He walks onto the building site, his thongs tug
through the mud. There is a block of land,
a pallet of bricks in the carpark of Walter Mart.

Tito Pat watches tomatoes grow

Fields are filled with bamboo crucifixes, strung with wire;
they're covered in vines, tomatoes hang like sins;
gravel has been turned to colour. When he twists
the leaves between his fingers they smell like ancient blood.

Tito Pat balances paper on rice

Tito Pat is here to read the sky,
to decide on building dates, to watch people
sign contracts with his hand. Each signature

is three meetings, a night without sleep
and half a ream of paper. Tito Pat knows
the dialect of currency; in his mind he covers
a field in sheets of paper. There's no breeze,
their words are marbled by the sun. Rice sways
beneath them, the paper floats; Tito Pat watches
paper rise, he lifts his palms, all this work
will house his family, will be paper
keeping the world from them.

Tito Pat reads the rice

On dark nights rice is graded in tin sheds,
the air is thick with starch, breath comes
in glutinous clumps. If the wind stirs,
tin squeals against itself. Chickens peck the dust,
machinery scrambles, a generator fills
the night with stutter. Tito Pat sits on a stool
his hand working through the grains
in a bucket before him. They slide
smooth against his palm.

Tito Pat lifts a Red Horse

People sit around him in shirts soured
with sweat. The sun has turned his family
to salt drifts, they move in clouds. His
day is spent with nets hanging from his fingers,
at nightfall the grains reform, familiar hands
emerge from the pillars of salt. Some nights
even the oldest of friends know where
he will be, they arrive with sheet music,
they arrive with excuses for holding
lovers by the neck, they arrive with blister
packs of prescription drugs. Tito Pat sits
with them all, listens with a Red Horse
at his lips. He hands them all a palmful
of rice; the angry among them crunch grains
between their molars, their spite sounds

like bones breaking. He must move
around the group, he knows they will disappear
before first light, he knows there are many people
to see, he knows the night will run where it runs.

Tito Pat eats dirt

There's a hothouse beside a concrete road,
power lines, grass pushing from the verge.
The plastic walls flap around him,
they talk to the breeze, they allow one
direction of wind. The bamboo struts rub
a song; they are filled with drops of recent rain.
The rain circulates, the rain moves into a heart;
Tito Pat licks the moisture from seedlings,
he imagines them twisting through a trellis
his tongue following, his tongue—
a lizard sliding through white roots. Every
mineral has a different flavour,
each crumb of soil is a story ready to be reborn.

Tito Pat in a bath of blood

Tito Pat has a field of fighting cocks,
shaded and bound to concrete slabs.
They scratch the dirt and beckon the sky,
they open wounds and drip blood
on their feathers, they drink sugar syrup
from terracotta pots. When they die he tears
their tough bodies into joints
and curries them. Tito Pat has a special recipe,
the pot must simmer for two days
in the hot sun, with everything stirred
each time the wind shifts. Their strength
keeps him blessed with purpose,
the meat fills him with feathered anger.

Tito Pat's last journey

Tito Pat eats gizzards from a stick,
when he digs his van out of a mudslide his family offer
to shape his hair with the sap from a rubber tree,
this is the closest he will come to being crowned.
He carries his guitar into the hills and communes with ancient
women who drip tattoos from their fingers.
In the forest he eats bugs and covers himself
in rainwater. Somewhere there is a horse
he should be riding, or one that will hold still
long enough for him to lay an ear against
its flank. The rain is incessant, the calamansi
drop as they pass. He listens
as his comrades talk about Haiyan—
a typhoon to name children after, a reason
to have wind carved on your arm.

Tito Pat lays himself to rest in the whip-tail of a monsoon,
embalmed with mud from the side of a mountain.
This is where he will fill the earth with weight,
listen as the world bellows imperfections,
dream in a way that suggests peace.

Corollary

Consequences arrive dressed in cargo pants,
phones and pistols weighing down their pockets. They stalk
through the streets like made men, tattoos on their necks,
rings clumped on fingers. We know them by name, recognise them
even when they don sunglasses. If they're at cafes before us
they always put a coffee on the tab; when we arrive
it's waiting. They know when we shop, where. Sometimes
we find them bagging fruit, hands on our yoghurt.
Some mornings they're sitting on the train
holding ultrasounds of our babies; it seems
to be a threat, except our children are grown.
They hold the sheets of film up against the window
and point. I don't know what happened to all our
children, for years they were hidden
behind the bedside table covered in dust.
When we get off the train our consequences muscle
after us. We don't run, we're resigned
to their company. I wonder how far they'll follow
us, how many years they'll commit to our tail.
If we'll book ourselves into an old folks home
and they'll be there pushing walking frames
and dribbling. Sometimes when we're having dinner
on a street-side table and they're lurking
in a doorway across the road, looking everywhere
but at us, I want to wave them over. Except I know
they're exactly what they appear to be, a hello
will turn brutal. They carry secateurs in their pockets.
A stray look could cost a finger.

Epistles

We're carrying epistles
Waking every morning
To a jug of cold water over our head
Shaving by streetlights

There are half-eaten bodies
Buried in the dirt
They've been shot in the neck
And we're dancing on the streets

Running up walls
Turning backflips with clerks
In their shirt sleeves
Our mothers are bedridden

Clutching their own hands
Every lover we've had is wearing
A different hat
Some of them have painted

Schnurrbärte on their lips
They're speaking in coughs
Eating fried eggs
And filling our arms with envelopes

russian steppes

/ our modern blood is amalgam /
animals and digital nightmares / growling and bleeping /
leaving shadows / strange symbols on skin /
when we wave to each other / there are logarithms
on our wrists / some days they're easy to see / changing / darker
as they morph into coordinates / postcodes / hours and places
hedging the air between us /

you tend them with creams / but noise
is unbreakable / each hour is a babble of numbers / bots / streaming
sites / places we've been / each footstep known and
digitally indexed / each number a new
name for the unfathomable / memory
a coded dream from the russian steppes /

we wake holding bloodlines against our ears /
our heart beating a calendar /
and places / coordinates growled by tigers /
years chittered by monkeys / there are anniversaries
alive in the numbers pushing from our veins /

one thousand times we drink from the same chipped cup /
whole suburbs move like leaves as we breath / when we want silence /
we drag our arms in waves / numbers turn to foam /
ciphers wash against our stomach /

Nine days

Medication is
    a tightrope. This
        line is something
            that could continue
                forever. I am nine days
                at 100mg and waiting to see
                what happens next. There are
                squadrons of leaves that appear
as I watch branches in the wind.
        There are greens that have
            forgotten their cousin yellow.
                Every time my phone vibrates
                it feels like a crocus pushing
                through dark soil. I answer it
                like an ode to summer.
        When I enter a room pollen
precedes me and when I leave
there's clover instead of
    footprints. People watch
        me from windows, people
            try to give sunlight a new
                name. I have been uneven
                    when I speak. It seems to be
                        the right volume, but
                people look at me like I've
                whispered. Everything I
            say has become a secret.
        I spend hours unravelling
            the code contained in a few
                syllables. Each word is a shadow cupped
                    in sunlight. I have been warned
                there will be days like this
                days like other days in which
            even this overturned world
                is overturned.

A Museum of Maybes

Parked cars outside falafel joints,
spit and tears on the ground.
The inner west is a Museum of Maybes
places that might have tuned a life
differently. There are captions below
every street sign. Blue plaques marking
the arguments we had, a glass box
holding all the wallets we lost,
your first phone. In the pub
      at the corner of our street someone has scratched
your favourite numbers in the jukebox glass—
        kids are always playing Radar Love.
          People have planted traffic lights
      instead of headstones in our memory:
posters peeling from the walls
remind us
there were nights when
      'to Plunder' was another way
        to say music.

Band shirt vespers

When we die let microphones spark
and feedback torture each amp,
make the band drop instruments and walk
from the stage. Around us bodies
will still and people will begin to speak;
all the good parts of us will emerge
from the woozy ooze a crowd makes swaying.
We will find our feet and walk
five centimetres above the ground.

When we die people will drop
black t-shirts in our coffins. Along one wall
there will be a list of all the bands we have seen.
People will mouth lyrics and play drums
against the air. No one will be allowed
to tell the truth. Even your name will be
wildly exaggerated, there'll be an overflowing
of letters, a howl of vowels. We'll be in every field
covered in mud, our eyes blinking
at the flashing lights. We'll bump shoulders
with sunsets as the crowd moves. When people sing
they will look for us, our open mouths will fill
with sky, and we'll shake last words
from the smoke living in our hair.

Songs for the after-party

We're stomping, sometimes arm in arm, we pretend
to live by moving our limbs, we put on
animal masks. There are deaths quaking within us.
We rattle them with each footfall—

three dead parents, music's lies, the holes
love hammers in a heart. We're gargling vodka
from the bottle, smashing cameras on the floor;
all that's held trapped within us empties

wild into the room, screaming, spitting on the floorboards.
Our mothers and fathers gush through us,
the living and dead; saviours, hair in raised rows
along their spines, they yell at us with rats in their hands—

tell us to dance, push words from our throats. They burn
like vodka in the cup of our stomach. We carry death's
half-life in our veins and it never clears
from our blood. We have seen too many wakes,

moving from tidy room to tidy room, listening as people
talk in tongues over their dead. Too many times
we have parked on the roadside, walked across gravel
to shake hands and kiss cheeks with people

standing in rows. We are silent when our tongues
are songs, waiting, thick with lyrics we don't know
how to sing. We watch walls, curtains swing,
brothers make speeches and we keep our hands

hidden in pockets. People we have eaten food with
stand in grey suits, if they're lucky a wind blows
through their hair. We only dance when all the dead
hum in unison. At the right time we can hear them—

and then we sing until the fear soars
from our scalps, we dance with heels of chalk
and when our mouth opens to scream it fills the dark
with every harmony we have ever known.

How long is too long?

Pollen drops from trees like a sweep of snow,
vegetal to the heart of itself, powdering
the air. I imagine my mother standing

beneath the trees. It's been so long,
the years have made her
transparent. All I can recognise is her shape,

pollen has settled
on her body. Countless golden pinheads
shift over her limbs. When she smiles

it's granular, a million particles of powder,
the intercession of a thousand flowers.

Echolocation

My daughter cradles a dying bat,
she consoles all creatures who fall from the sky.

I have shopping in my arms, a loaf of bread,
peaches, yoghurt. My mind is only daylight

and there are dusk's creatures dying,
wings crumpled—coughing, cat-like final breaths.

The eyes open and close, teeth flare
pale at the sky; somewhere this mammal

is still in ragged formation, the world
moving in a series of reflected sounds.

My daughter and I are hollow
vibrations. She places the creature carefully

on the grass, this will be a daylight death.
I kneel beside her. She bends close to the bat

and whispers, pushing a last breath
into the gaping mouth, 'I remember all your songs.'

Spare keys

In the future my daughter will love
and that will be enough. Blood will flow
under her skin. The hounding daily news
will be a source of fleeting fear. She will

concoct plans to upend this world. Her friends
will message too much, they will carry discontent
far into the future; it will be temporarily
glorious. We will say goodbye through car windows

as we rush to other people and places—and it will
be enough. Every message she sends will be
without punctuation, and if I read them closely
they will run together, they will be a procession

of days, and, even a single word will be enough.
One day she will come to me asking for spare keys
to her flat. I'll find them in my drawer,
we'll walk over to her place. On the way we'll

talk about the nights we spent bound to bad
television, waiting for B-listers to reveal scores.
Really we'll be talking about something else,
we'll be saying—I'm well. How are you?

We'll be hovering around each other
with memories. I'll be using my right hand
to shade the sun, she'll be wearing sunglasses,
and it will be enough to pretend I'm too lazy

to walk up her stairs. She'll appear at the window
above and call my name. I'll edge around and wait
for her to drop the keys in my hands. Cars will
pass on the street behind me. This will be

true and possible. She will wave from the window,
she will say—see you later. A bus will pass,
somewhere a tree will grow new leaves—
uncountable trees and their uncountable leaves,

learning to live again, learning to fill us
with their air. I will stand, looking up
as she draws back through the open window.
I will think of the endless shades of green,

all the edges of leaves, fronds, needles
making their way into the world, and it will
be enough, it will help us to breathe.

Afterword

Every poem in this collection has a face I know, a voice and a body. They walk the streets and meet each other, they have conversations, they mingle and discover intentions, they recognise what the other poems have lived through. They are poems within a family history, within a history of companions, poems of a time and a place. They're individuals in the larger world they make together. They have their own histories and their own stories. If these poems are trying to do anything it is to recognise the human in each other, to feel what the other poems have been through. And, to recognise the human and humane in the people who read them. They have hollows that are listening, that are yielding enough to be filled by the life others bring to them. They are trying to be their most human selves, trying to live as well as they are able.

Acknowledgements

Cath, you are a new world every day, thank you for your love and curiosity. The fierce faith you have in words helped me to believe it was possible to write the poems in this collection.

To the people who find their shadows in these poems, thank you.

Thanks to Recent Work for trusting this book and thanks to Penelope Layland for editing the collection.

Felicity Plunkett, Bilal Hafda and Caitlin Maling, thank you for your endorsements; it's a pleasure to share this collection with such wonderful poets.

I respectfully acknowledge that this book was written on the land of the Gadigal, Dharug and Whadjuk peoples.

No gin in the afternoon contains the words 'blind giant dancing' these were borrowed from the title of Stephen Sewell's play The Blind Giant is Dancing

Dancing at the Bone Bank contains descriptions of the osteoconduction process drawn from the 'Bone grafting' Wikipedia page

Thanks to the following publications and prizes for the love they've shown poems in this collection: *Overland, Montreal Poetry Prize, Val Vallis Poetry Prize, Cephalo Press.*

About the Author

Rico Craig is a writer, workshop facilitator and award-winning poet whose work melds the narrative, lyrical and cinematic. His poetry has been awarded prizes or shortlisted for the Montreal Poetry Prize, Val Vallis Prize, Newcastle Poetry Prize, Dorothy Porter Poetry Prize and University of Canberra Poetry Prize. BONE INK (UWAP), his first poetry collection, was winner of the 2017 Anne Elder Award and shortlisted for the Kenneth Slessor Poetry Prize 2018. Since 2012 he has worked as Storyteller-in-Chief at the Story Factory, designing and facilitating creative writing programs for young people, and teacher development programs for adults.

Printed in Australia
Ingram Content Group Australia Pty Ltd
AUHW020941220724
397340AU00002B/18